KING FOR A WEEK

T0359658

Written by Max Greenslade

Illustrated by Ian Forss

Flying Start
to Literacy®

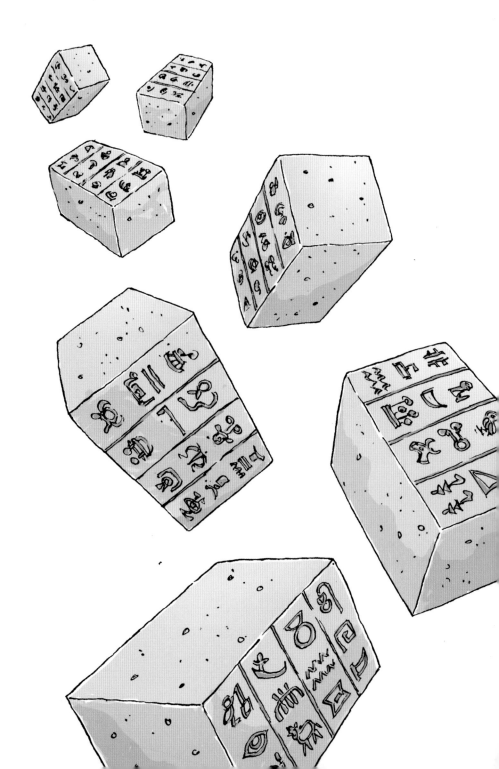

CONTENTS

Chapter 1

A HORRIBLE NIGHTMARE

"My pyramid!" roared the king as he sat bolt upright in his bed. "My pyramid! It is a disaster!"

The king's voice boomed throughout the palace. A tall man pattered down the sandstone hallway, followed by a dozen servants. As they approached the king's bed, the servants bowed and lay on the floor, arms outstretched. The tall man remained standing and lowered his head towards the king.

"What seems to be the matter, my king?" asked Menkhaf, with a slight sigh in his voice.

The king looked troubled and his brow was covered in sweat. Menkhaf nudged one of the servants with his foot. The man got up and scuttled away, returning with a clay pitcher and a copper cup. He poured water into the cup and bowed, giving it to the king.

The king slapped it away.

"Get out! Get out, all of you!"

The servants got up and, walking backwards and bowing, went quickly out of the room.

"Menkhaf, I had a terrible dream!" cried the king.

"Was it about your pyramid again?" asked Menkhaf, soothingly.

The king nodded, then he became angry.

"Those lazy builders! They were not working fast enough! In my dream, I was old and my pyramid was not built. I won't have it!" yelled the king, bringing his fists down on his knees.

"It was just a dream, my king," said Menkhaf. "I have been to the pyramid myself. The builders are working hard, just as you ordered."

The king threw back the silk covers and jumped out of bed.

"I must see the pyramid myself, now!"

Menkhaf clapped his hands loudly three times. In an instant, the servants were back in the room with a selection of beautiful robes for the king to choose from.

The king waved them away.

"I want to wear peasant clothes. If I go as myself, the Great King of Egypt, I will not see what is truly going on. The builders will pretend to be hard at work if they see their king watching. I will see the truth if they don't know it's me."

He pointed to one of the servants.

"Get me some clothes like his!"

The servant quickly found some clothes and passed them to Menkhaf.

The king looked with disgust at the simple garment, then he barked, "Get a boat ready. We are leaving immediately. I want no warning. No one is to know we are coming, or you will pay with your lives."

Chapter 2

AT THE PYRAMID

"Where are the fishers? Why are they not fishing?" demanded the king as they sailed down the Nile River towards the pyramid. "I want fish for my dinner tonight!"

"The fishers are working on the pyramid as you commanded," said Menkhaf. "Everyone in the kingdom is working on the pyramid."

As they rounded the bend in the river, the king and servants gasped as they saw the pyramid before them, rising up from the desert.

"By Horus, it is immense! But they are nowhere near finished! Hurry, get my litter ready. I want to see why those lazy peasants are taking so long," said the king.

"But, Your Majesty, you must walk behind. You cannot travel in your royal litter dressed as a servant," Menkhaf reminded him.

So the king, disguised as a lower rank servant, walked behind, while Menkhaf rode in a litter decorated in the style of a high-ranking official.

On the way, they passed workers who were carrying tools and ropes. As they got closer, they heard the ringing sounds of hammers hitting chisels and the shouts and groans of thousands of workers.

Gangs of workers were hauling stones towards the pyramid. At the base of the pyramid, stood a tall, wooden crane that was struggling to lift a heavy stone. The king was silent as he took in the majestic scene.

Not far from the crane, a stonemason was removing a wooden mould from a newly-cast block of stone. A crowd was watching him. He hit the hammer precisely. Suddenly, the mould came away to reveal a perfect block of stone, and the crowd cheered.

"Well made, Sebu. You have such skill," said one of the workers standing nearby, admiring Sebu's stone. "Why have you left your sarcophagus business in Memphis to work here?"

"I had no choice," said Sebu, shrugging his shoulders. "Like everyone else here, I have been ordered by the king to work on his pyramid."

"We will be back home soon enough," said the worker. "As soon as the pyramid is finished."

"We will never finish this pyramid," said Sebu.

The worker frowned. "What do you mean?"

"Look around you. The workers are weak and exhausted. The stones are big and heavy, and many of them are not well cut so they do not fit together." Sebu pointed to the pyramid where a crane was lifting a stone.

"And the crane is not strong enough to carry those stones to the very top of the pyramid. I have been trying to see the chief engineer for weeks to advise him of a better way to work. We could be making some of the stone blocks up on the pyramid. Also . . ."

Sebu was suddenly cut off from the workers as the litter carrying Menkhaf approached. The king, dressed as a servant, walked behind.

The king stumbled forwards and came face-to-face with Sebu. They stared hard at one another as the crowd gathered around.

"What? No, it couldn't be!" the king gasped.

But yes, Sebu the stonemason looked exactly the same as the king! It was like looking in a mirror.

"Stop!" shouted the king. "Where is that man? Where did he go?"

He looked around angrily, but Sebu had disappeared into the crowd.

"Who, Your Majesty?" asked Menkhaf, wearily.

"That man I just saw. He looked just like me. I will find that man, and I'll have him charged with treason. He's an impostor!"

But the king's words were drowned out by the groans from the huge group of workers that was trying to lever a massive stone out of the ground with long pieces of timber.

A man stood over them and cracked his whip. "Heave! Heave, you sluggards!"

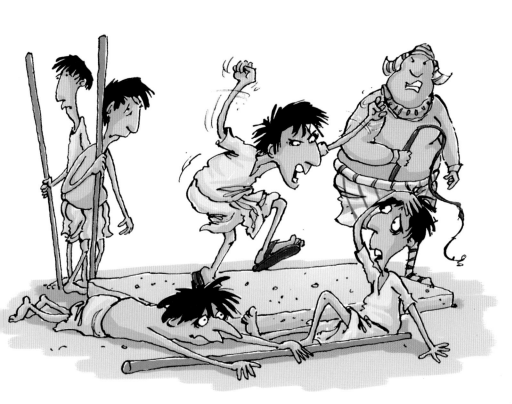

The workers desperately tried to push down on the timber to lift the slab of stone out of its hole. Suddenly, two of the workers collapsed and the stone landed with a thump back in the ground.

"Get up! Get up, you lazy peasants!" screamed the king, forgetting that he himself was dressed as a peasant.

The man with the whip looked over at the king in surprise.

"I'm the one giving orders around here. You get back to work yourself, you lazy peasant!" And he cracked his whip.

"Your Majesty, you should not draw attention to yourself," said Menkhaf quietly. "Remember, you are disguised as a peasant."

"Well, why is everyone so lazy? Look at them!" said the king accusingly, gesturing to the thousands toiling slowly in the hot sun.

"They are hungry. They have not eaten today. The crops are not being harvested, so there is little to eat. They only have one meal each day. And they are working without rest," said Menkhaf. He took a deep breath. "The workers are suffering, Your Majesty, when they are being forced to work under these conditions."

"Forced to work? I am their king! It is an honour for the people of Egypt to build my pyramid!"

A cry of alarm interrupted the king.

"What now?" he yelled.

A huge stone had broken loose from its ropes and was sliding down the ramp towards the workers.

Hundreds of workers dropped their tools and began to run, right towards where the king and Menkhaf stood.

The king gasped in horror as the horde of workers ran towards him. He turned and began to run too. He was soon swallowed up in the crowd, disappearing from sight.

Chapter 3

THE LOST KING

Menkhaf and the palace servants looked everywhere for the king, but he had disappeared. They could not call out for him and they could not ask for help. Apart from Menkhaf and the palace servants, no one knew that the king was dressed as a peasant. And all the peasants were dressed the same.

A crowd had gathered around a worker who had collapsed on the ground. Menkhaf pushed his way through, hoping it would be the king. People parted for the tall, well-dressed man. Menkhaf breathed a sigh of relief. It was the king!

"What happened to this man?" Menkhaf demanded from the crowd. "Who did this?"

A worker spoke up. "I think he just fainted, sir."

"Stand back!" Menkhaf picked up the unconscious king. "Servants, we leave now. Hurry!"

The servants jogged towards Menkhaf with his litter. As he laid the king on the litter, the crowd murmured incredulously: "A peasant in a litter?"

The servants picked up the litter and carried the king back to the boat moored on the river.

On the boat, the unconscious king was gently placed on a pile of feather cushions. Menkhaf washed the dust from him with a cool wet cloth and a servant dressed the king in clean robes.

Menkhaf chuckled when he thought about how the king had run from the crowd. He had not seen him run like that since he was chased by a monkey as a small boy.

Sebu stirred on the bed and opened his eyes. Where was he? He looked around. He was on a beautiful boat. He was clean and he was dressed in fine silk robes.

Standing next to the bed was a tall man.

"Ah, thank goodness you are awake, Your Majesty," said the tall man. "I think perhaps that it was too much for you to go in disguise to the pyramid, dressed as a peasant. Do you feel all right now?"

Sebu grunted. His mind whirled. This man thinks I'm the king! He would have to play along. If he was caught out, it would be the end for him and his family!

"Yes, much better. I think I may have had a bit too much sun."

"Your voice sounds different, Your Majesty," said Menkhaf, concerned. "Perhaps it was all the dust? Are you ready to go back to the palace?"

"The palace?" said Sebu in alarm. If they went back to the palace, then his charade would be discovered.

"No, no, we must stay here. I need to go back to the pyramid today." An idea quickly formed in his mind.

"I want to see the chief engineer. I have an idea about how to finish the pyramid."

Menkhaf looked at Sebu in surprise. "Really? Your Majesty has an idea?"

Sebu decided that he should act like a king.

"Yes, an idea. And if you want to stay out of the dungeons, then you will take me to the chief engineer NOW!"

Menkhaf nodded and clapped for the litter to be brought immediately.

When Menkhaf and Sebu arrived at the chief engineer's house, the guards shouted: "All hail the king. The king is here."

In the courtyard of the house, a man was sitting at a table eating a sumptuous feast, as a group of musicians played their instruments.

When the chief engineer saw Sebu dressed as the king, he jumped up out of his chair.

"Your Majesty, such an honour," said the chief engineer, bowing low.

"How is it that you are sitting here eating while my pyramid slowly becomes a disaster?" shouted Sebu. He was enjoying shouting at the chief engineer, who had been refusing to see him for weeks.

"Your Majesty, I can assure you that I have been working hard," said the chief engineer. "I am merely taking a short break."

"But I have seen it," said Sebu. "I have seen the badly cut stones. The stones do not fit together properly. The whole project is a catastrophe!"

"Your Majesty, I . . ." began the chief engineer.

"Stop!" commanded Sebu. "I have an idea for completing the pyramid. You will follow my orders or you can enjoy the rest of your life in the dungeons!"

"Of course, Your Majesty. I would be honoured to obey," said the chief engineer, bowing with nervous relief.

Menkhaf looked at the king in surprise. How quickly he had learnt about building pyramids!

Chapter 4

THE REAL KING

Meanwhile, the real king had been wandering around the pyramid for hours looking for Menkhaf.

"You there! What do you think you're doing?"

The king turned around. Hopefully, it was Menkhaf. But no, it was the ferocious man with the whip he had seen earlier. The king kept walking. Suddenly he was grabbed from behind.

"Are you ignoring me? Got somewhere better to be, have you?"

The man with the whip held the king by the arm and pushed him towards a group of workers.

"Now, get down there and get that stone out of the ground, you lazy peasant!"

The king opened his mouth to shout at the man. Then he saw the man raise his whip, and he closed it again.

"Now, heave!" And the man cracked the whip.

The king, together with the other workers, pushed down on the timber, and slowly the stone lifted up out of the ground. It was hard working under the hot sun. Dust covered every bit of him and his muscles ached. His soft hands were raw and blistered, and he was desperately thirsty and hungry. He dared not ask for a drink, as he was terrified of the man with the whip.

"When do we eat?" the king asked the worker next to him.

The worker snorted. "We only get one meal a day, at the end of the day when we're finished. According to the king, that's all we need. He's a tyrant! If he was here right now, I'd punch him on the nose!"

The king gasped in shock. He was about to shout at the man, but decided not to. The man might punch him!

He had to get away and find Menkhaf.

When the man with the whip was busy yelling at another worker, the king dropped to his knees and crawled away.

"Hey! You there! Come back! Where do you think you're going?"

The king felt two strong arms around him.

"Trying to escape are we?"

He turned quickly. It was a guard.

"Get your hands off me!" ordered the king.

"Oh, all high and mighty are we?" shouted the guard. "A few days in prison will sort you out!"

And he pushed the king in front of him, as they trudged through the dust towards a row of buildings.

A week later, the king was finally let out of prison. The guard walked him back to the pyramid to begin work again.

"Will I be hauling stones again?" asked the king.

"No, it's all changed. The king has issued new orders. No more cutting, no more hauling. They are making the blocks up there on the pyramid. It's brilliant!" said the guard.

"The king?" asked the king. "How can that be?"

"Simple," said the guard. "He's the king!"

Chapter 5

A GLEAMING PYRAMID

When they reached the pyramid, the king was astonished. The pyramid had grown taller. Everywhere he looked, the king saw groups of workers singing and talking as they worked.

One group of workers was mixing together powdered stone with water. Another group was shovelling the mixture into baskets and carrying it up a ramp that wound its way around the outside of the pyramid. The workers poured the mixture into wooden moulds. When the mixture was hard, the workers broke the wooden mould to reveal a block of stone – the same way Sebu had been making the blocks of stone at the base of the pyramid.

In the distance, the king saw Menkhaf talking to a man who was holding a sheet of papyrus. The man, who was pointing and explaining something, looked strangely familiar.

"Menkhaf!" yelled the king and waved. "Menkhaf! Over here!" Menkhaf heard the king's voice. He looked over, but all he saw was a grubby peasant waving and running towards him. He turned back to his discussion.

"Menkhaf!" yelled the king again.

The guards ran up to the king and grabbed him. "What are you doing, you peasant? Get back to work!"

"I am the king!" he shouted. "Menkhaf, tell them who I am!"

Menkhaf shook his head. "Listen, peasant, this is the king right here."

Menkhaf pointed at Sebu, who looked nervous. Then Menkhaf looked from one to the other, and gasped. It was true. Sebu was not the king. No wonder his voice sounded different!

"What's going on here?" asked Menkhaf.

"My name is Sebu," said Sebu. "I am a stonemason and I have been trying to talk to the chief engineer for weeks, but he wouldn't listen to my advice."

"Arrest this impostor!" shouted Menkhaf.

"I didn't mean any harm," yelled Sebu. "I just wanted to help finish building the pyramid. Please don't put me in prison!"

The king looked at Sebu. "Yes, you're right, I won't put you in prison."

"Thank you, Your Majesty," said Sebu with relief.

"Prison is too good for you! Hand back my royal robes before I feed you to the crocodiles instead!"

The guards took off the king's robes and dragged poor Sebu towards the river.

The king watched them for a moment, then turned to Menkhaf.

"I've had a terrible week, Menkhaf. I was treated like a common peasant, even a criminal. I was whipped, and beaten, and thrown in prison. And all the while, you were letting that impostor pretend to be me!"

"Please believe me, Your Majesty," said Menkhaf, as he placed the royal robes on the king, "I had no idea that man was an impostor." He bowed low. "But look at your pyramid, Your Majesty. It has grown quickly in the last week. It will be finished quite soon, probably in time for your birthday."

The king's eyes gleamed. "Really? That soon?" The king forgot all about his terrible week and clapped his hands. "Where is the chief engineer? I must speak to him."

The chief engineer bowed low in front of the king.

"This is brilliant work, chief engineer. What made you change the way you are building it?" the king asked.

"Well, Your Majesty, I was thinking while I was working – you know how hard I work."

"Yes," said the king. "Tell me how you thought of your idea."

Menkhaf looked at the chief engineer sternly. "Tell the king the truth. Who is responsible?"

"Well, you know I wondered if perhaps, it might be faster if we, um . . ."

Just then, a worker came to the king and bowed.

"Your Majesty, we need your help with the pyramid. Some of the workers are arguing about the measurements for the ingredients to make the blocks of stone. Only you know the formula."

The king turned to the chief engineer. "So, it was not your idea at all, but the impostor's! Where is he?"

"You sent him to be fed to the crocodiles," said Menkhaf, calmly.

"Well don't just stand there! Let's go and get him!"

They reached the river just as Sebu was walking into the water. Guards stood with their spears pointing at him. Crocodiles were swimming towards Sebu.

"Stop! Stop!" shouted the king. "I command you to stop! It is because of you, impostor. You are the one who has made it possible to build my pyramid so quickly!"

Sebu bowed, trembling with relief. "I only wanted to serve Your Majesty the best way I could. I did not mean to pretend to be you, Your Majesty."

The king looked Sebu up and down. "I don't know how they could have made a mistake. You don't really look like me at all. You're not nearly so handsome!"

Sebu nodded. "Of course, Your Majesty. You know I never meant to . . ."

The king held up his hand. "Let's just forget it, shall we? Now we must get back to the pyramid. As the new chief engineer, you are needed desperately."

The chief engineer was fired in disgrace, and Sebu was promoted in his place. He was richly rewarded when the pyramid was completed in time for the king's birthday.

Once the pyramid was built, Sebu returned happily to his sarcophagus business in Memphis. He hoped that he would never have to work on another pyramid again!